Cambridge ICT Starters

On Track Stage 1

Third Edition

Jill Jesson and Graham Peacock

CAMBRIDGE
UNIVERSITY PRESS

CAMBRIDGE
UNIVERSITY PRESS

4381/4 Ansari Road, Daryaganj, Delhi 110002, India

Cambridge University Press is part of the University of Cambridge.

It furthers the University's mission by disseminating knowledge in the pursuit of education, learning and research at the highest international levels of excellence.

www.cambridge.org
Information on this title: www.cambridge.org/9781107625198

First published 2003
Second edition 2005
Third edition 2013

Printed in India by Shree Maitrey Printech Pvt. Ltd., Noida

A catalogue record for this publication is available from the British Library

ISBN 978-1-107-62519-8 Paperback

Additional resources for this publication at www.cambridgeindia.org

Cambridge University Press has no responsibility for the persistence or accuracy of URLs for external or third-party internet websites referred to in this publication, and does not guarantee that any content on such websites is, or will remain, accurate or appropriate. Information regarding prices, travel timetables, and other factual information given in this work is correct at the time of first printing but Cambridge University Press does not guarantee the accuracy of such information thereafter.

· ·

· ·

Introduction

Cambridge ICT Starters: On Track, Stage 1 has been written to support learners who are following the Cambridge ICT Starters syllabus. It follows the syllabus closely and provides full coverage of all the modules. The sections of the book correspond to the modules and follow the order in which the modules appear in the syllabus. The book builds on creating and formatting documents featuring text, images and tables; planning, creating and organising multimedia presentations, incorporating audio and animation effects; designing and creating, testing, modifying and evaluating spreadsheets and graphs; and creating, developing and testing databases, whilst maintaining data security.

The book provides learners and their helpers with:

- examples of activities to do
- exercises for practice
- instruction in using their computers
- optional extension and challenge activities

It is designed for use in the classroom with coaching from trained teachers. Where possible the work has been set in real situations where the computer will be of direct use. The activities are fairly sophisticated yet simple enough to be followed by adults as well as children!

Some exercises require the learners to open prepared files for editing. These files are available to teachers on www.cambridgeindia.org website. The website provides useful graphics and templates for creating pictograms. Some pictures and text files are also included to help young learners so that they can learn editing without first creating the files required.

The activities in this book use Windows 7 Operating System and Microsoft Office 2007 software. However, the syllabus does not specify any particular type of software in order to meet the learning objectives.

Please note that when learners view the screen shots contained in this book on their computer screens, all the type will be clearly legible.

Contents

Module 1
Documents for a Purpose

Learning Objectives

	Student is able to:	Pass/Merit
1	Create and format text which is suitable for a particular purpose	P
2	Adjust properties to allow graphics or other objects to fit well within the document	P
3	Insert table into document	P
4	Use advanced formatting features	M
5	Use page formatting options	M
6	Adjust page formatting for a specific audience	M

Who will be reading?

- Before you format your text, think of the audiences who will be reading it.
    - How do you attract them to read?
    - How do you make your text more appealing to them?
- Consider the audiences according to:
    - age
    - occupation
    - background
    - interest.
- Vary the format by changing:
    - font styles
    - text sizes
    - colours
    - images.

- Children will like:
    - colourful text
    - little text
    - simple colour graphics or illustrations
    - easy-to-read font style
    - big text size.
- Young people are more concerned with:
    - moderate font size
    - stylish font style
    - colours
    - attractive illustrations.
- Older people may prefer:
    - big text size
    - simple font style
    - useful and relevant illustrations.

Typing and formatting text

- Type the following article.
- Use spell-checker to check for spelling errors.
- Proofread to ensure the whole text is typed correctly.
- Save it in your folder as launchingcis.

Launching of Cambridge ICT Starters in Mukah, Sarawak, Malaysia. The Information and Communication Technology (ICT) programme at SK Dato Awang Udin in Mukah, Sarawak, Malaysia was launched by former Prime Minister Tun Dr Mahathir Mohamad on 10 April 2004. The ICT programme, which will witness the introduction of 'Cambridge ICT Starters' for students at the school, marks yet another important milestone for the spread of ICT education to rural schools, especially in the coastal belt. The ICT programme is a pilot project for Mukah and the coastal area, and is an extension of an earlier successful pilot project which was launched at SK Datu Pengiran Mohamad, Oya, another rural area, by Sarawak Chief Minister Pehin Sri Dr Haji Abdul Taib Mahmud in 2001. The ICT project will complement the Government's efforts in bridging the digital divide between the rural and urban areas and eradicating rural poverty. Describing the ICT education project as an important enabler in promoting IT-assisted learning, the company's managing director, Kuintan Sepawi, said, "We like to consider our contribution from the private sector as one which is supportive of the Government's k-economy initiative, which seeks to move Malaysians away from physical resources towards knowledge-based resources." On the Cambridge ICT project, she said it highlighted the various critical components necessary in creating a sustainable ICT-focused education programme.

Changing font

- Open the file launchingcis.
- Find out what the default font of your word processor is.
- Hold **Ctrl** and tap **A** simultaneously.
- If the default font is Calibri, then change the font of the text to Times New Roman; otherwise change the font of the whole passage to Calibri.
- Calibri or Times New Roman are two very common fonts that are easily accepted by most audiences.

- You may wish to select a different font. Whatever font you have chosen, make sure it is suitable for your audience.

Choose the font from the list.

Changing font size

- Find out what the default font size of your word processor is.
- Hold **Ctrl** and tap **A** simultaneously.
- If the default font size is 11, change it to a bigger size of 14.
- Now try to change the font size to 16.
- Change the font size back to 11.
- Font size 11 is a very common font size and is suitable for adults.
- Children and older audiences may prefer the bigger font size of 16 or even 18.

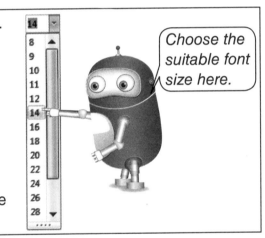

Choose the suitable font size here.

Text alignment

- Place the cursor anywhere in the text.
- Click ≣, the text will be aligned at the centre.
  Titles are usually aligned at the centre.
- Click ≣, the text will be left aligned. If the page width or column width is limited, left alignment is a better choice.
- Click ≣, the text will be right aligned. Date and page number are commonly right aligned.
- Click ≣, the text will be justified. Justified text looks neat and professional.

Centre aligned

Right aligned

Left aligned

Justified

Formatting the title

- First align all the text as Justify.
- The first line can be taken as the title of the story.
- Place the cursor at the end of the first line, to the right of the full stop.
- Tap [Backspace ←] once to remove the full stop.
- Tap [←Enter] twice to separate the title from the rest of the text.
- Place the cursor anywhere within the title.

- Click [≡] to make the title centre aligned.
- Highlight the title.
- Click [B] to make the title **bold**.
- Click [U] to underline the title.
- Change the font size of the title to 14.
- Change the font style of the title to Century Gothic or any legible font.
- Change the font colour to red.
- Click [💾] to save the file using the same filename.

Break the text into paragraphs.

- Highlight the whole text and change the font size of the body text to 12.
- The body text is too long and therefore difficult to read.
- We can break the text into a few paragraphs.
- Each paragraph should discuss one main point.
- Place the cursor on the left of the first word of the text: 'The'.
- You may tap [Tab ←→] once to insert an indent to the first paragraph, but this is not necessary.
- Identify the third sentence: 'The ICT programme is a pilot project...'

- Place the cursor on the left-hand side of the first word of the third sentence: 'The'.
- Tap [←Enter] once.
- This breaks the third sentence from the second sentence.
- Tap [←Enter] again.
- This will insert a blank line.
- Tap [Tab ←→] to insert an indent for the second paragraph.
- Click [💾] to save the file using the same filename.

Another paragraph

- Identify the fourth sentence of the newly formed second paragraph: 'Describing the ICT education project undertaken ...'
- Place the cursor to the left-hand side of the first word: 'Describing'.
- Tap [←Enter] twice.
- This will create a new paragraph and insert a new line above the new paragraph.
- Tap [Backspace ←].
- This will remove the blank line if you have not typed anything on it.

- Tap [←Enter] again to insert a blank line above the third paragraph.
- You may tap [Tab ←→] to insert an indent for the third paragraph.
- Click [💾] to save the file using the same filename.
- Click [⊞], hover over [🖨 Print] to see [🔍].

Click [🔍] to preview what your document looks like.

1.3 Inserting images

More formatting

- Locate and highlight the school name 'SK Dato Awang Udin' in the first paragraph.
- Change the colour to deep blue.
- Locate the following names and change their colour to deep blue:
  - Tun Dr Mahathir Mohamad
  - Pehin Sri Dr Haji Abdul Taib Mahmud
  - Kuintan Sepawi
- Locate 'Cambridge ICT Starters' in the first paragraph and change its colour to red.
- Click 💾 to save the file using the same filename.

Launching of Cambridge ICT Starters in Mukah, Sarawak, Malaysia.

The Information and Communication Technology (ICT) programme at SK Dato Awang Udin in Mukah, Sarawak, Malaysia was launched by former Prime Minister Tun Dr Mahathir Mohamad on 10 April 2004. The ICT programme, which will witness the introduction of 'Cambridge ICT Starters' for students at the school, marks yet another important milestone for the spread of ICT education to rural schools, especially in the coastal belt.

The ICT programme is a pilot project for Mukah and the coastal area, and is an extension of an earlier successful pilot project which was launched at SK Datu Pengiran Mohamad, Oya, another rural area, by Sarawak Chief Minister Pehin Sri Dr Haji Abdul Taib Mahmud in 2001. The ICT project will complement the governments efforts in bridging the digital divide between the rural and urban areas and eradicating rural poverty.

Describing the ICT education project as an important enabler in promoting IT-assisted learning, the company's managing director, Kuintan Sepawi, said, "We like to consider our contribution from the private sector as one which is supportive of the Government's k-economy initiative, which seeks to move Malaysians away from physical resources towards knowledge based resources." On the Cambridge ICT project, she said it highlighted the various critical components necessary in creating a sustainable ICT-focused education programme.

Inserting images

- A relevant image often explains the meaning better than words.
- Click on Insert tab.
- Click 🖼️.
- Select the image drmahathir.jpg.
- The image will be inserted at the position of the cursor.
- You can move the image or resize it.
- Place the cursor at one of the four corners.
- The shape of the cursor changes to ⬉. Drag it inward to reduce or outward to enlarge the image.

Drag diagonally to enlarge or reduce the image.

Moving the image

- Click anywhere on the image.
- Once the image is selected, the Format tab is displayed.
- Click 📷 Text Wrapping.
- Try out the different text-wrapping properties one by one to see the effect on the text around the image.

- Finally, choose square as the text-wrapping property.
- Place the cursor anywhere inside the image.
- The shape of the cursor changes to ✥.
- Drag to move the image to a new position.

More images

- Click on Insert tab.
- Click .
- Select the image oya.jpg.
- Resize, change text wrapping to square and place it somewhere in the second paragraph.
- Insert another image pic2.jpg, resize, change text wrapping to square and place it somewhere in the third paragraph.
- Click 💾 to save the file using the same filename.
- Close the file.

World's Longest Bridge Spans

- Click 📄 to start a new document.
- Type the following heading:
  World's Longest Bridge Spans
- Change the font style to Times New Roman.
- Change the text size to 24.
- Align the title at the centre ▤.
- Add the following text:
  Longest Bridge Spans are categorised in the following tables according to the structural type of the main span. The 'span' means the main span of a bridge = centre-to-centre distance of adjacent towers, pylons, piers or supports given in metres. It does not mean the total length or overall length of multi-span bridges. Overall lengths are not included - only the longest spans. 'Year' means the year of completion or intended completion if known.
- Set the font size to 12.
- Set the alignment to Justify ▤.
- Save as longestbridge in your own file folder.

Inserting a table

- Make sure the cursor is placed at the end of the document you have just typed.
- Tap ⏎ Enter twice.
- Type 1. Suspension Bridges
- Click on Insert tab.
- Click ▦ Table.
- Click ▦ Insert Table....
- In the dialogue box, change the number of columns to 6 and the number of rows to 2.

1.4 Tables

Typing in the tables

- Type the heading of each column.
- Tap `Tab ⇄` to move to the next column.
- When you reach the last cell, tapping `Tab ⇄` again will insert a new row.

No.	Bridge	Span (m)	Location	Country	Year

- Adjust the column width by dragging the border of the column.
- Place the cursor on the border until it changes its shape to ‖.
- Hold down the mouse and drag to the left or to the right to resize the column.
- Complete the table so that it looks like the sample below:

1. Suspension Bridges

No.	Bridge	Span (m)	Location	Country	Year
1	Akashi-Kaikyo	1991	Kobe-Awaji	Japan	1998
2	Xiahoumen Bridge	1650	Zhoushan Archipelago	China	2009
3	Great Belt East	1624	Hasskov-Sprogo	Denmark	1998
4	Yi-Sun-Sin	1545	Gwangyang-Yeosu	South Korea	2012
5	Runyang South	1490	Yangtze River	China	2005

More tables

- Add the following two tables:

2. Cable-Stayed Bridges

No.	Bridge	Span (m)	Location	Country	Year
1	Russky	1104	Eastern Bosphorous Strait	Russia	2012
2	Sutong	1088	Suzhou-Nantong	China	2008
3	Stonecutters	1018	Rambler Channel	Hong Kong	2009
4	E-dong	926	Huangshi	China	2010
5	Tatara	890	Seto Inland Sea	Japan	1999

3. Steel Arch Bridges

No.	Bridge	Span (m)	Location	Country	Year
1	Chaotianmen	552	Chongqing	China	2009
2	Lupu	550	Shanghai	China	2003
3	New River Gorge	518	Fayetteville,WV	USA	1977
4	Bayonne	504	New York	USA	1931
5	Sydney Harbour	503	Sydney	Australia	1932

- Click 💾 to save the file.

Numbering

- Click [ ] to start a new blank document.
- Type the following text:

Everybody likes to blow out the candles on the birthday cake during his or her birthday party. Candles create a special atmosphere on this special occasion. Candles are handy too when there is power failure.

Treat the candles well; they bring you joy and happiness. Treat them carelessly; they bring fire into your home!

Here are some guidelines on candle safety:

Double-check they're out when you do not need them.
Keep clothes and hair away from them.
Keep children and pets away.
Put them on a heat-resistant surface.
Put them in a proper holder.
Keep them away from inflammable materials like curtains.
Take care with votive or scented candles.
Use a snuffer or a spoon to put them out.
Don't put them under shelves.
Don't move them when they're burning.
Don't leave them burning while you are out.
Don't keep candles too close to each other.

Formatting

- Save the document you have just typed in your folder as: candlesafety.
- Read through the document once again carefully to ensure that you did not miss out any words.
- Use a spell-checker to check for spelling errors.
- Click [ ] to save the document again if you have made any changes.
- Insert a title for the document: CANDLE SAFETY.
- Set the font for the title to Arial.
- Set the font size to 16.
- Make the title **bold**.

- Set the alignment to centre [≡].
- Highlight the guidelines starting from 'Double-check they're out when you do not need them.' up to the end of the document.
- Click [≡▾].
- Notice that all the guidelines will be numbered from 1 downwards.
- Click [≡▾] again.
- The numbering has disappeared.
- Now click [≡▾].
- Instead of numbering, the guidelines are listed one by one after a bullet.
- Clicking [≡▾] again will toggle off the bullets format.

Formatting numbering

- Instead of numbering the guidelines 1, 2, 3, 4, ... etc., we can change the format to A, B, C, ...

- Highlight the guidelines again.

- On the Home tab, click on ▾ beside 🔢 ▾.

- Click on one of the styles listed.

- You can repeat the commands for a different style.

- Click 💾 and save your work before you proceed.

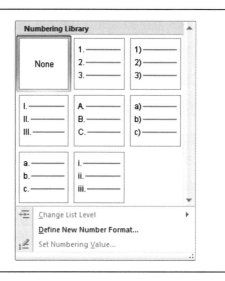

Formatting bullets

- As with numbering, bullets can be changed.
- Highlight all the guidelines.
- On the Home tab, click on ▾ beside 🔢 ▾.
- Click on the styles of bullet of your choice.
- Repeat the commands to see the effect of different bullets.
- Click 💾 to save the document.

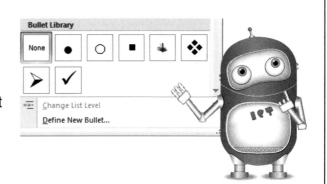

Customised bullets

- Click on ▾ beside 🔢 ▾.

- Click on Define New Bullet... .

- Click Font... and select a font of your choice, click OK .

- Click Symbol... and select a new character of your choice, click OK .

- Click Picture... if you prefer to have different pictures as bullets, click OK .

- You can try out the text position, indent, tab space and so on, as well.

- Click OK when you have finished.

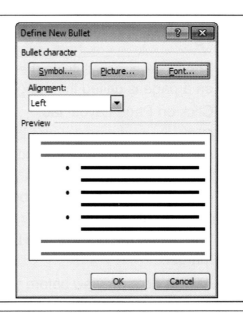

1.6 Page setup

Page orientation

- Click  to open the file candlesafety.

- Click on Page Layout tab.

- Click Orientation ▼ .

- Under Orientation, click Landscape .

- Click on View tab, click One Page to see what Landscape Orientation looks like.

- Repeat for Portrait orientation: Portrait .

- Click on View tab, click One Page to see what Portrait orientation looks like.

This is Portrait orientation.

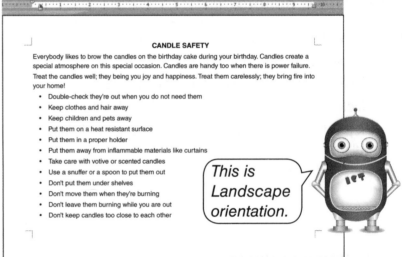

This is Landscape orientation.

Margins

- The blank space outside the printing area on a page is called the margin.

- Click on Page Layout tab.

- Click Margins and click the icons in turn to see how they affect your text.

- Click Custom Margins... . Click ▲ to increase or ▼ to decrease the top, botom, left or right margin.

- The bigger the number, the bigger the margin.

- Always do a preview before you print.

Paper size

- You must also check the size of the paper that you will be using.

- Click on Page Layout tab.

- Click Size ▼ .

- Check the paper size.

- If you are using single sheet, select the most common size, A4, from the list of sizes.

- If you are using continuous computer paper, select letter.

- Always do a preview before you print.

Changing a document

- You are the secretary of the school Science Club. You are asked to change an article so that it is suitable to be put on the Science Club's bulletin board.
- Open the file tallestbuilding.
- Make the following changes to the heading (The Tallest Building in the World) of the document:
  - Text size: 16 point
  - Font colour: blue
  - Insert a blank line after the heading.
  - Font: Tahoma
  - Alignment: centre
- Make the following changes to the sub-heading (The ten tallest buildings in the world):
  - Text size: 14 point
  - Font: Arial
  - Alignment: centre
  - Font style: Bold and Italic
  - Font colour: green
  - Insert a blank line after the sub-heading.
- Make the following changes to the body text of the document:
  - Text size: 12 point
  - Font: Times New Roman.
- Insert a blank line after the line, 'After the completion of Taipei 101, the other 10 tallest buildings in the world are': and number the items under it.
- Insert bullet points to the 4 categories for measuring tall buildings so that they look like this:
  - height to the structural or architectural top
  - height to the highest occupied floor
  - height to the top of the roof
  - height to the top of the antenna.
- You may use a different shape for the bullets.
- Insert a blank line after the last paragraph.
- Insert the following text and table after the blank line:
  In fact if we just measure them all from bottom to top, building or not, cables or not, public facilities or not, a ranking of the tallest structures in the world would look like this:

Category	Structure	Country	City	Height (metres)	Height (feet)	Year Built
Skyscraper	Burj Khalifa	United Arab Emirates	Dubai	829.8	2,722	2010
Self supporting tower	Tokyo Sky Tree	Japan	Tokyo	634	2,080	2011
Guyed Mast	KVLY-TV mast	United States	Blanchard	628.8	2,063	1963
Clock tower	Abraj Al Bait Towers	Saudi Arabia	Mecca	601	1,972	2011
Tower for scientific research	BREN Tower	United States	Nevada Test Site	462	1,516	1962
Mast radiator	Lualualei VLF transmitter	United States	Lualualei	458	1,503	1962

- Adjust the column width, if necessary.
- Save your file as tallestbuildingworld.

Insert images

- With the help of your teacher, obtain images of Taipei 101, Kuala Lumpur Petronas and Sears Towers.
- Insert the image of Taipei 101 on the right-hand side of the first paragraph. Insert the image of Kuala Lumpur Petronas on the left-hand side under the third paragraph.
- Insert the image of Sears Tower to the right of the image of Petronas.
- Adjust the size of the images and the text-wrapping properties so that the whole document covers only 2 pages.

- Insert page numbers at the bottom right of the pages.
- Insert a header which has:
  - your name on the left-hand side
  - the date in the middle
  - your school name on the right-hand side
- Use Arial font of size 10 point for the header.
- Proofread the document and make corrections, if necessary.
- Save your document as tallestbuilding2.

For the magazine

- Your document has been selected for the school magazine so that all the pupils can read it.
- You are now required to refine your document on page formatting, page orientation, colours, location of inserted images, font, font sizes and so on, to make it more appealing and appropriate for its audiences (your schoolmates).
- Save your work as tallestbuilding3.

Self-evaluation

- Explain the choices you have made when creating your document, which make it suitable for its purpose.

_____

_____

_____

_____

_____

_____

_____

_____

_____

Optional extension and challenge activities

Module 1 – Documents for a Purpose

Challenge 1 ⟩

- Write a letter to a friend which tells them what you have done over the past year.
- Justify your address to the right. Centre the date and justify the main text to the left.
- List the three most enjoyable things you have done and bullet the list.

Challenge 2 ⟩

- Write a one page newsletter to explain what has happened in your school during the term. Tell people about the sports and music in the school as well as the lessons.
- Add pictures of some events.
- Use Text Wrap to tightly fit the pictures into the text.

Optional extension and challenge activities

Challenge 3

Create a strip cartoon of a favourite story.

- Insert a 4 x 3 table into an MS Word document in horizontal page format.
- Put ten returns into lines 1 and 3, and two returns into lines 2 and 4.
- Add speech bubbles to the wide rows with text to show what people are saying.
- Type text in rows underneath to tell the story.
- Print and add pictures by hand.

Module 2
Multimedia for a Purpose

Learning Objectives

	Student is able to:	Pass/ Merit
1	Create a plan for a presentation	P
2	Recognise and select appropriate source materials	P
3	Incorporate transition and animation	P
4	Incorporate timings, audio and 'build' effects	M
5	Demonstrate a clear sense of audience and purpose	M

Planning

- When you decide to do a presentation, you must start with planning.
- First, you need to identify the theme of your presentation.
- Next, you need to identify your audience.
- Plan your slides and think how your presentation can attract your specific audience.
- Gather resources like information, graphics and sound or music files.
- Select the relevant resources and organise them on a storyboard.

- You can apply your skills in word processing to prepare your storyboard or you can just scribble your ideas on a blank piece of paper.
- Your storyboard is then your master plan for the presentation.
- You must revise your master plan from time to time.

You must know what your audiences want.

Storyboard

- Start MS Word with a blank page.
- Use the textbox feature to create 7 identical textboxes.
- Name the textboxes Slide 1 to Slide 7. For the exercise that you will go through in this module, let us prepare a presentation for the members of the School Science Club (the audience) on 'World Record – the animal extreme' (the theme).
- As there are a few thousand world records, we will use a small category, 'The largest', for the presentation.
- In the textbox for Slide 1, type the title as

World Record – The Animal Extreme.

- On the second line, type The largest ...
- At this point, do not worry about the format.

> Slide 1
>
>
> World Record —
> The Animal Extreme
>
>
> **The largest ...**

Preparing the slides

- Open the file animalextreme.docx.
- For exercise purposes, the file has been prepared with some information on some world records.
- Identify the information that is relevant to the topic.
- Copy the information on the largest flying mammals.
- Paste it in the textbox for Slide 2.
- The slides need spacing out on the screen so they can all be seen.

> Slide 2
>
> Largest Flying Mammals – The Flying Foxes (family *Pteropodidae*)
> - Live in Southeast Asia.
> - Length of 45 cm (17.7 in).
> - Wingspan – 17 m (5 ft 7 in).
> - Weight – 1.6 kg (3.5 lb).

2.2 Preparing the storyboard

Other slides

- Identify the next data that show 'the largest ...'.
- Copy and paste the information to form Slide 3.
- Discard those data that are not relevant.
- Repeat the copy and paste process.
- There are all together 6 pieces of information that show the largest, and therefore there should be altogether 7 slides.

- Save your storyboard.
- To identify your file quickly later on, use your name as part of the filename: e.g. if your name is John, then save your work as john'ssbwr.

Images and sound

- As part of the planning, identify the images that you would use in the presentation and write them down on the storyboard.
- You can insert 1 or more images.
- All the images selected must be relevant or related to the presentation.
- The illustration should help the audience to gain a better impression of the information presented.
- You can also identify a sound file to be played throughout the presentation to make the presentation even more interesting.

> Slide 2
>
> Largest Flying Mammals – The Flying Foxes (family *Pteropodidae*)
> ○ Live in southeast Asia.
> ○ Length of 45 cm (17.7 in).
> ○ Wingspan – 1.7 m (5 ft 7 in).
> ○ Weight – 1.6 kg (3.5 lb).
> Graphics: flyingfox.jpg, flyingfox2.jpg, flyingfox3.jpg

The filenames of the graphics need not be shown in the presentation.

Getting started

- Click  to open Start menu.
- Click ▶ **All Programs**
- Click Microsoft Office PowerPoint 2007 .
- Click on Design tab.
- Choose between a blank presentation and an appropriate design template.
- Click on the sample design on the Themes group and the starting slide will be changed to the design selected.

I have selected Technic.pot. You may choose your own design.

Title slide

- Create the first slide as the title slide.
- Click on the space marked 'Click to add title'.
- Type the title as World Record - Animal Extreme.
- On the Home tab, click A to increase or click A to decrease the font size so that the title stretches over only 1 line.
- Move the title to the top.
- Click on the space marked 'Click to add subtitle'.
- Type The Largest ... .
- Adjust the font size.
- Add your name below the subtitle.

The second slide

- On the Home tab, click New Slide.
- If you have created the storyboard using MS Word, you can copy the title and paste it into the box marked 'Click to add title'.
- You can click on it and type out the title.
- Check your spelling and resize the wordings.
- Change the colour of the title to yellow.

Completing the slide

- Click at the area marked 'Click to add text' and complete the text as in your storyboard.
- Click on Insert tab.
- Click Picture.
- Select the image that you think is relevant.
- Resize and move the image if necessary.
- You can insert more than 1 image.
- Save your presentation as animalextreme.

The other slides

- Based on the storyboard you have created, complete the other 5 slides.
- The screen shots shown here are just examples.
- You are encouraged to rearrange the images or move the text.
- While designing the slides, you must always bear in mind who your target audience is.
- Save your work before you leave your computer.

Largest Fish – The Whale Shark (*Rhincodon typus*)

- Plankton-feeding
- Found in the warmer areas of the Atlantic, Pacific, and Indian Oceans.
- Length – 12.65 m (41 ft 6 in).

Slide 5

Largest Bird – The Ostrich

- Live in North African.
- Height – 2.75 m (9 ft).
- Weight – 156.5 kg (345 lb).
- Also the fastest bird on land – it can run up to 72 kmph (45 mph).
- It can't fly!

Slide 3

Largest Mammal – The Blue Whale (*Balaenoptera musculus*)

- Length – 35 m (115 ft).
- Weight – 130 tonnes.

Slide 6

Largest Reptile – the estuarine or saltwater crocodile (*Crocodylus porosus*)

- Live in India.
- Length – over 7 m (23 ft) long.

Slide 4

Largest Insect – Acteon Beetle (*Megasoma acteon*)

- Found in South America.
- Length – 3.5 in.
- Width – 5.1 cm (2 in).
- Thickness – 3.8 cm (1.5 in).

Slide 7

2.3 Slide transition

Slide show

- Open the presentation animalextreme.pptx that you saved in the previous exercise.
- Make sure that you are looking at the first slide.
- Click on Slide Show tab.
- Click  .
- Left-click your mouse anywhere on the screen to advance to the next slide.

You can also tap the space bar, [→] or [↑] to advance to the next slide. Tap [↓] or [←] to reserve to the previous slide.

You can click the [⬚] icon located at the bottom right corner to start the slide show too!

Transition

- To advance the slides in a more attractive way, we can add in slide transition.
- Click on Animations tab.
- Choose one of the transition methods by clicking at it once.
- Click on to view the transition.
- Repeat the choosing of slide transition methods for all other slides.
- Click on Slide Show tab.
- Go back to the first slide and click From Beginning to go through the presentation again.

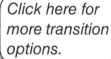

Click here for more transition options.

Speed and sound

- For each slide transition, you can choose the speed: slow, medium or fast.
- You can also choose a sound effect.
- After you have made the choices, go back to the first slide and click [⬚] Preview to have a preview of the effects.
- Click [💾] to save the presentation.

2.4 Automated presentation

Auto advance

- At this point, you still need to advance to the next slide manually by clicking the mouse or by tapping the space bar, → or ↑ .
- You can produce an automated presentation whereby the slides will be advanced automatically after a specified period of time.
- Look for Advance Slide under the Animations tab.
- Uncheck the option ☐ On Mouse Click .
- Check the Option ☑ Automatically After: .
- Click ▲ repeatedly to increase the timing to 5 seconds.

- Click Apply To All .
- Make sure you are viewing the first slide.
- Click From Beginning to run the show.

You can also type in the timing manually.

Animation

- You can use animation to change the way in which the images or texts are displayed.
- Click on Animations tab.
- Click Custom Animation .
- On Slide 1, click to select the title.
- Click Add Effect ▾ .
- Select Entrance ▸ .
- Choose 5. Fly In or any other effect.
- Click ► Play to have a preview.

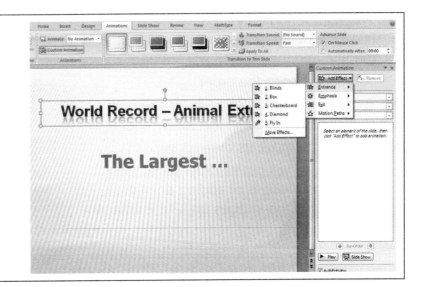

Text animation

- Repeat the animation for the subtitle The Largest ... .
- You can choose the same or a different entrance effect.
- Click ► Play to have a preview.
- Try out other effects one by one so that you are familiar with each of them.
- Choose the one that you think your audience will like.
- Repeat for all the titles of the other 6 slides.
- Click ⊟ to save your work.

Graphic animation

- Select Slide 2.
- Click on one of the inserted graphics.
- Click on Animations tab.
- Click [Custom Animation].
- Click [Add Effect ▼].
- Select [Entrance ▶].
- Choose [More Effects...] to see more entrance effects.
- Click [Box] or any other effect.
- Click [► Play] to have a preview.
- Repeat the process for other images.

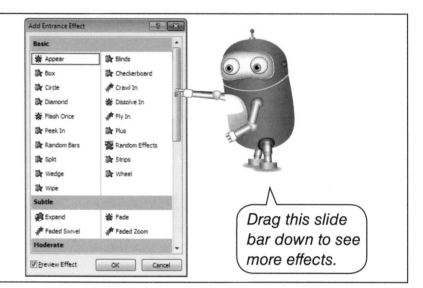

Drag this slide bar down to see more effects.

Re-order

- The numbering that appeared next to the title and the images show the order that the title and the images will appear.
- You can change the order.
- To swap the order 3 and 4, for example, click the third effect in the Task Pane.
- Click [⬇] to move its order down.
- Clicking [⬆] will put its order back. Now repeat the process of adding animation effects to all the images on all the other 6 slides.

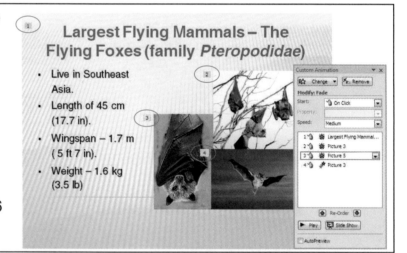

Build effect

- The body texts that are already in the bullets format can be set to appear one by one.
- This is called the build effect.
- Follow the procedure above to apply effects to each line.
- Select [Entrance ▶].
- Click [More Effects...] to select more entrance effects.
- Select [Crawl In].

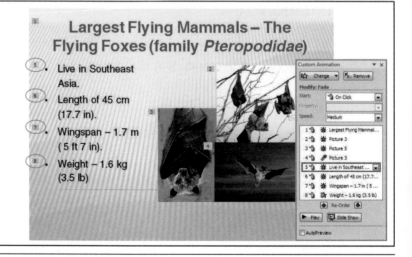

Change setting

- Click ⯆ on the right of

  Start: | ⏱ After Previous ⯆ | and

  choose After Previous to ensure a smooth
  automated presentation.

- Click ⯆ on the right of Direction: | From Bottom ⯆ |
  to select a direction on entrance for the text
  from a list of directions:

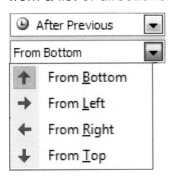

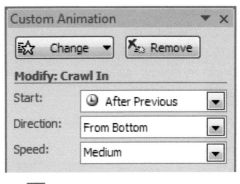

- Click ⯆ on the right of

  Speed: | Medium ⯆ | to choose

  a speed from the list.

The text contents

- The animation properties are listed
  in the Custom Animation pane. Click

  Custom Animation to see or hide the list.

- Click 💾 to save your work before you
  proceed to set the animation of the texts of
  other slides.

Although it is a thrill to watch the animations, overdoing it will only confuse the audience and distract their attention. Keep your work simple.

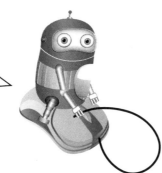

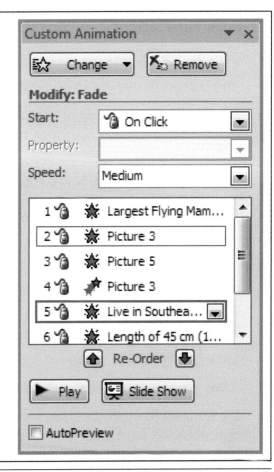

Inserting Music

- Go to slide 1.
- Click on Insert tab.
- Click on ▾ below **Sound** .
- Click ◀ **Sound from File...** .
- Choose the midi sound champions
- Click **OK** .

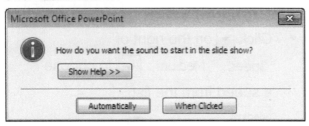

> To ensure that the music can be played during the presentation, the music file must be kept in the folder where the presentation file is saved, whether it is saved on the hard disk, diskette, CD or any other storage devices.

- Click **Automatically** to allow the sound to play automatically in the slide show.

Control how the music is played

- In the Custom Animation pane, click ▾ on the right- hand side of ⏲ ▷ Kalimba.mp3 ▾ .

- Click **Effect Options...** .

- This will open the Play Sound dialogue box.

- For this exercise, we want to play the music from the beginning until the end of the slide show.

- Select ⦿ **From beginning** under **Start playing** .

- Select ⦿ **After:** 7 ▴▾ **slides** under **Stop playing** and type 7 as we have 7 slides.

- Click 🔊 under Sound Setting to activate the volume control and drag the handle up and down to control the volume of the music when it is played.

- Click **OK** to complete the setting.

- Save your work and test-run the slide show.

- If you need to make adjustments, remember to save your work again.

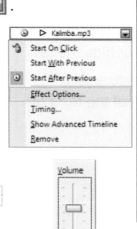

Rehearse timings

- To ensure that the slide show created is suitable for the target audience, especially the timings, you can rehearse it.
- Click on Slide Show tab.
- Click  .
- The slide show will start automatically from the first slide with a timer.

- When you reach the end of the slide show, a dialogue window telling the total time recorded will be displayed.
- Click [Yes] to accept and keep the recorded time.
- Save your work.
- Test-run the slide show.
- You can repeat the rehearsal or change the timing manually in the Task Pane.
- Imagine that you are the target audience who will be watching the slide show.
- Tap the space bar whenever you think the title, the photos, the text or the whole slide should change to the next one.

Slide transition timing

- You can still change the speed of slide transitions.
- In the Animations tab, Transition to This Slide group, for speed, choose Fast, Medium or Slow.

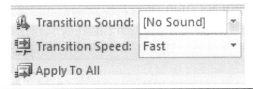

- You can also choose a sound effect.
- In the Transition to This Slide group, under Advance Slide you can change the time lapse before the next slide advances.

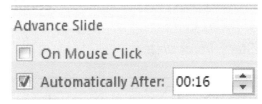

Change the timing of animation effects

- In the Custom Animation pane, select the effect to change.
- Click ▼ .
- Click Timing... .
- Choose [After Previous ▼] for Start: This will start the effect after the specified time in Delay:
- Specify 0 seconds in Delay:. This will start the effect immediately.
- Choose a Speed from: 0.5s (Very Fast), 1.0s (Fast), 2.0s (Medium), 3.0s (Slow) or 5.0s (Very Slow).

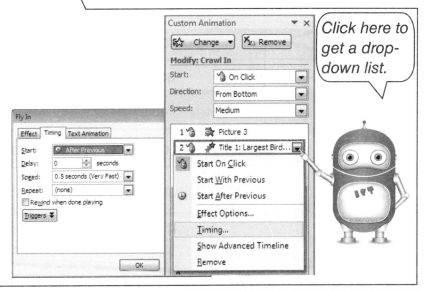

Resizing notes window

- For documentation purposes, you can add notes to each slide.
- You can note the transition and animation effects you have used for each slide.
- Bring your mouse pointer I to the bottom of the work place of the slide.
- Move it between the slide work place and the window labelled Click to add notes until it changes its shape to ⇕.
- Hold the right button of the mouse and drag it up or down to resize the window for writing notes.

Drag here up and down to resize the textbox for writing notes.

Writing notes

- For Slide 1, type the following notes:
  - Slide transition: *Blinds*
    - Direction: *Horizontal*
    - Speed: *Fast*
    - Advance slide: *Automatically after 2 seconds*
  - Animation used for the title: *Dissolve In*
    - Start: *Immediately*
    - Speed and duration of animation: *Very Fast (0.5s)*
  - Animation used for the subtitle: *Spiral In*
    Speed and duration of animation: *Fast (1.0s)*
  - Music: *champions.mid*
    Start: *From the beginning*
    Stop: *After 7 slides (the last slide of the slide show)*

Notes for Slide 2

- The following are examples of notes for Slide 2:
  - Slide transition: *Box In*
    - Speed and duration: *Fast (1.0s)*
    - Advance slide: *Automatically after 15 seconds*
  - Animation for title: Blinds
    - Direction: *Horizontal*
    - Speed and duration: Very Fast (0.5s)
  - Animation for photo — flyingfox: *Fly In*
    - Direction: *From Top*
    - Speed and duration: *Very Fast*
  - Animation for photo 2 — flyingfox2: *Peek In*
    - Direction: *From Bottom*
    - Speed and duration: *Very Fast*
  - Animation for photo 3 — flyingfox3: *Wedge*
    - Speed and duration: *Medium*
  - Animation for bulleted text: *Crawl In*
    - Direction: *From Bottom*
    - Speed and duration: *Medium*
- Follow these examples and write similar notes for your own Slide 2 and the other 5 slides.

2.8 Printing

Notes Page view

- You can also type the notes using Notes Page view.
- Click on View tab.
- Click Notes Page.
- Type your notes in the textbox under the slide.
- You can also resize the slide and resize the textbox to allow for more notes.
- To return to normal view, click on View tab.
- Click Normal.

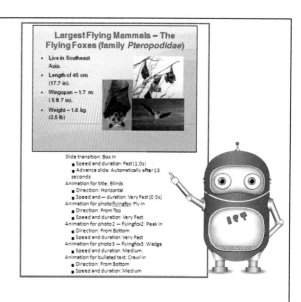

Printing

- Click 🔵 to open Office menu.
- Click 🖨 Print ▸.
- There are 4 types of printing: Slides, Handouts, Notes Pages and Outline View.
- Select the type of printing under Print what: and click Preview to preview how the pages will look before you start printing.
- Select Slides if you want to print each slide one by one.
- Select Handouts if you want to give out hard copies of the slides to your audience.
- You can select to print 1, 2, 3, 6 or 9 slides on a single page.
- Select Notes Pages if you want to print the notes slide by slide.
- Select Outline View if you want to print all the text without the images.

Make sure the printer is on-line before you click OK to start printing.

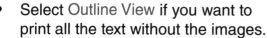

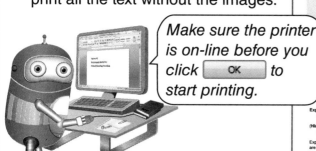

Notes Page

Outline View

Handouts

Evaluation

- After the completion of the slide show or presentation, view it as a slide show a few times with your target audience and think of ways in which you can improve your slide show.
- Write down as documentation why and how your slide show meets its purpose and how appealing it is to your target audience.
- The following questions will help you to evaluate your slide show. Write your answers in complete sentences. You can always write your own observations.

  ○ Explain how the background chosen suits the title of the presentation.
  (*Hints*: *Background used is globe; the title is about world records*)

  _____

  ○ Explain why the font styles and the font sizes used are suitable.
  (*Hint*: *Are they simple and legible?*)

  _____

  ○ Explain how the use of music from the beginning to the end of the show helps to impress the target audience.
  (*Hints: How suitable or related is the music chosen to the title of the presentation? How did the audience react to the use of music during the presentation?*)

  _____

  ○ Explain how the use of photos helped in the presentation.
  (*Hints: Are they relevant and related to the topic presented? Are they informative? Have the inserted photos made the presentation more interesting?*)

  _____

  ○ Explain the role played by the timings set.
  (*Hints: Are the timings well set? Did the audience have sufficient time to finish reading? Were longer times allowed for longer text?*)

  _____

  ○ Explain how the use of transition of slides and animations helped in the presentation.
  (*Hints: Did the use of transition of slides and animations make the presentation more interesting? Did the build effects on the texts make the text easier to comprehend or understand and make the presentation more impressive?*)

  _____

Optional extension and challenge activities

Module 2 – Multimedia for a Purpose

Challenge 1

Plan a multimedia presentation for a tourist attraction or holiday destination you would like to visit.

- Make the presentation as exciting as you can.
- Use text boxes or plain paper to plan the way the screens will link together.
- Insert some hotel adverts in a 'Where to Stay ' section.
- Search the Internet for relevant pictures.
- Make a bulleted list of the best things to see.

Challenge 2

- Find out about the snacks your friends like. Do they prefer fruit, chocolate, nuts or biscuits as part of a snack?
- Plan and create a multimedia presentation about a snack you have invented.
- Use transitions and animations to make your presentation interesting.

Optional extension and challenge activities

Challenge 3

- Plan and create a multimedia presentation set out like a magazine about the Olympic Games.
- Choose maps, pictures, text and sound files to interest the reader.

Module 3
Spreadsheets for a Purpose

Learning Objectives

	Student is able to:	Pass/ Merit
1	Design a spreadsheet with a specific purpose	P
2	Create the spreadsheet	P
3	Test the spreadsheet	P
4	Modify the spreadsheet to make it suitable for its purpose	M
5	Evaluate the spreadsheet	M

Sell and buy

- Mrs Teo wants to trade-in her present old car for a new car. She has three main criteria to consider:

  ○ The monthly loan repayment instalment must not be more than $600 and the duration must not be more than 7 years.

  ○ The trade-in price must not be less than $7000.

  ○ The down-payment payable after deducting the trade-in price must not be more than $5000.

- She has five offers but cannot make up her mind.

Which car is the best buy?

Designing a spreadsheet

- Design a spreadsheet to help Mrs Teo answer her question:

  ○ Which offer best suits her needs and criteria?

- You will start by deciding the column headings of the spreadsheet.

- The following are the main column headings that you need to consider:

  (a) Offer (for Car A, B, C, D and E)

  (b) Price of new car (for listing the price of the new car from the 5 offers)

  (c) Minimum down-payment (as set by the offer)

  (d) Trade-in price (for listing the trade-in price of the old car)

  (e) Down-payment payable (the minimum down-payment minus the trade-in price)

  (f) Principal loan (price for new car – down-payment)

  (g) Duration of loan (in years)

  (h) Rate of interest (in %)

  (i) Total interest payable (duration of loan x rate of interest)

  (j) Total amount payable (principal loan + total interest payable)

  (k) Monthly instalment (total amount payable ÷ (duration of loan x 12))

Labelling the spreadsheet

- Load ![Excel icon] Microsoft Office Excel 2007.

- A blank spreadsheet is displayed.

- Key in the column headings as shown.

- Save the spreadsheet in your own folder as Teo'scarloan-design.

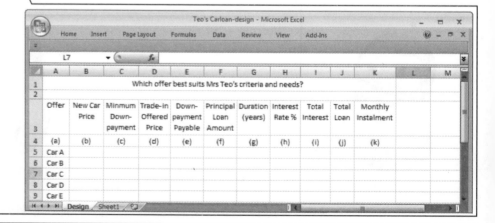

3.2 Formulas

The offers

- According to Mrs Teo, the five offers are as follows:
  - Offer 1 (Car A)
    - Price of new car: $42 000
    - Trade-in price: $9000
    - Minimum down-payment: $10 000
    - Duration of loan: 5 years
    - Interest rate: 3.35% per annum
  - Offer 2 (Car B)
    - Price of new car: $48 350
    - Trade-in price: $10 000
    - Minimum down-payment: $10 000
    - Duration of loan: 6 years
    - Interest rate: 3.30% per annum
  - Offer 3 (Car C)
    - Price of new car: $45 000
    - Trade-in price: $8000
    - Minimum down-payment: $10 000
    - Duration of loan: 7 years
    - Interest rate: 3.20% per annum
  - Offer 4 (Car D)
    - Price of new car: $32 000
    - Trade-in price: $7500
    - Minimum down-payment: $15 000
    - Duration of loan: 4 years
    - Interest rate: 5.0% per annum
  - Offer 5 (Car E)
    - Price of new car: $38 000
    - Trade-in price: $6500
    - Minimum down-payment: $8000
    - Duration of loan: 8 years
    - Interest rate: 3.0% per annum

Entering available data

- The worksheet designed has 11 columns but the information on the offers can only be used to fill up 6 of the columns, (a), (b), (c), (d), (g) and (h).
- Open the file Teo'scarloan-design.xlxs.
- Fill up the 6 columns (a), (b), (c), (d), (g) and (h) with the data from Mrs Teo.
- Check the data that you have entered carefully; adjust the column width, if necessary.
- Save your work as Teo'scarloan-data.xlxs.
- Discuss with your friends on how to use appropriate formulas to calculate the values for columns (e), (f), (i), (j) and (k).

Keying-in the formulas

- Formula for Column (e): Down-payment Payable (e) = Minimum Down-payment (c) minus Trade-in Offered Price (d).
  - Click to select cell E5.
  - Tap [=].
  - Click cell C5.
  - Tap [−].
  - Click D5.
  - Tap [←Enter].
- Cell E5 will only display the value of the formula; the formula is displayed at the formula bar above the first row.
- You can also type the formula =C5-D5 directly into cell E5.
- You can repeat the process to key-in a similar formula for cells E6, E7, E8 and E9.
- To save time, you can use the Copy and Paste method:
  - Click cell E5.
  - Click [icon].
  - Highlight cell E6 to cell E9.
  - Click [icon].

Columns (f) and (i)

- Formula for Column (f): Principal Loan Amount = New Car Price (b) – Minimum Down-payment (c).
  - ○ Click to select cell F5.
  - ○ Tap [=].
  - ○ Click cell B5.
  - ○ Tap [–].
  - ○ Click cell C5.
  - ○ Tap [←Enter].
- Copy the formula to cells F6, F7, F8 and F9.

  *MS Excel only recognises * instead of x as multiplication.*

- Formula for Column (i): Total Interest = Principal Loan Amount (f) x Duration (g) x Interest Rate (h).
  - ○ Click to select cell I5.
  - ○ Tap [=].
  - ○ Click cell F5.
  - ○ Tap [*].
  - ○ Click cell G5.
  - ○ Tap [*].
  - ○ Click cell H5.
  - ○ Tap [←Enter].
  - ○ Copy the formula to cells I6, I7, I8 and I9.

Column (j)

- Formula for Column (j): Total Loan = Principal Loan Amount (f) + Total Interest (i).
  - ○ Click to select cell J5.
  - ○ Tap [=].
  - ○ Click cell F5.

  - ○ Tap [+].
  - ○ Click cell I5.
  - ○ Tap [←Enter].
  - ○ Copy the formula to cells J6, J7, J8 and J9.

Column (k)

- Column (k) is the most important column and the formula = J5/(G5*12) must be entered with care.
  - ○ Click to select cell K5.
  - ○ Tap [=].
  - ○ Click cell J5.
  - ○ Tap [/].
  - ○ Click cell G5.
  - ○ Tap [( ].
  - ○ Click cell G5.
  - ○ Tap [*].

  MS Excel only recognises / as the symbol for division.

  - ○ Type 12.
  - ○ Tap [ )].
  - ○ Tap [←Enter].
  - ○ Copy the formula to cells K6, K7, K8 and K9.
- Save your spreadsheet as Teo'scarloan-data2.

*J5/(G5*12) means cell J5 divided by the product of G5*12. J5/G5*12 means cell J5 divided by cell G5; the dividend is then multiplied by 12.*

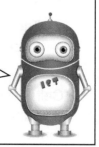

Testing the formulas

- Are the formulas working correctly?
- Test the spreadsheet by changing some of the data.
- If the down-payment is the same as the new car price, there will be no loan, no interest and no instalment.
- Change the value of C5 to 42 000 (the same amount as B5): are all the values for cells F5, I5, J5 and K5 zero (or –, depending on the format used)?
- If your answer for the above is 'yes', the formulas for columns (f), (i), (j) and (k) are working; if not, check to see that you have entered them correctly.

- To check the formula for column (e), change the value of the minimum down-payment (c) to 0.
- If the formula for column (e) was entered correctly, when there is no minimum down-payment (c), the down-payment payable (e) should show a negative value. The value is the same as the trade-in offered price, column (d).

	A	B	C	D	E	F	G	H	I	J	K	L
1				Which offer best suits Mrs Teo's criteria and needs?								
2												
3	Offer	New Car Price	Minmum Down-payment	Trade-in Offered Price	Down-payment Payable	Principal Loan Amount	Duration (years)	Interest Rate %	Total Interest	Total Loan	Monthly Instalment	
4	(a)	(b)	(c)	(d)	(e)	(f)	(g)	(h)	(i)	(j)	(k)	
5	Car A	42000.00	42000.00	9000.00	33000.00	–	5.00	3.35%	–	–	–	

Design Sheet1

Change the value of (c) to the value of (b), then the value of (f), (i), (j) and (k) will become 0 or –.

	A	B	C	D	E	F	G	H	I	J	K	L
1				Which offer best suits Mrs Teo's criteria and needs?								
2												
3	Offer	New Car Price	Minmum Down-payment	Trade-in Offered Price	Down-payment Payable	Principal Loan Amount	Duration (years)	Interest Rate %	Total Interest	Total Loan	Monthly Instalment	
4	(a)	(b)	(c)	(d)	(e)	(f)	(g)	(h)	(i)	(j)	(k)	
5	Car A	42000.00	–	9000.00	9000.00	–42000.00	5.00	3.35%	7035.00	49035.00	817.25	

Design Sheet1

Change the value of (c) to 0, then the value of (e) will be the negative value of (d).

3.4 Displaying formulas

Displaying the formulas

- Click on Formulas Tab.

- In the Formula Auditing group, click
  Show Formulas to see the formulas in the spreadsheet. Click the icon again to see the values.

- Save the file under the same filename Teo'scarloan-data2.

- Repeat the process to display the formulas again.

- Adjust the column width to fit the content of each column.

- Save the spreadsheet as Teo'scarloan-formulas.

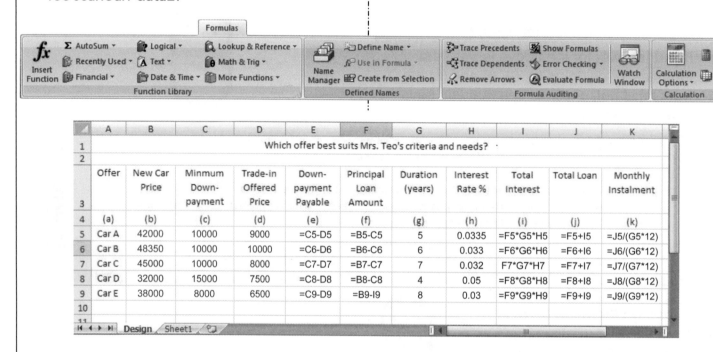

Interpreting the findings

- Based on the calculation, the monthly instalments are as follow:
  - Car A $622.67
  - Car B $638.10
  - Car C $510.00
  - Car D $425.00
  - Car E $387.50

- Only Cars C, D and E meet Mrs Teo's first criterion that the monthly instalment should not be more than $600.

- Car E cannot be considered because its trade-in price offered, $6500 is less than Mrs Teo's request of $7000.

- Car D seems to be a good choice but the down-payment payable of $7500 is over the limit set by Mrs Teo.

- It is, therefore, obvious that the only offer that best answers the question:
  Which offer best suits her needs and criteria?
  is Car C.

3.5 Graphical presentation

A different presentation

- To present the findings in a more friendly and more convincing way, you can show the results by using a column chart.

- Open the file Teo'scarloan-data2.xlxs.

- Highlight cells A5 to A9.

- Hold down the Ctrl key.

- Highlight cells K5 to K9.

- On the Insert tab, click .

- Select the Column graph.

- To enter the following labels click the Layout tab. Click Chart Title ▾ and choose position of the title. Add title text. Click Axes and add labels.

    ○ Title: Monthly Instalment

    ○ Category (X) axis: Offer

    ○ Value (Y) axis: Amount in US$

- Place the completed chart under the data table.

- Draw another two column charts with appropriate titles and labels for Down-payment Payable and Trade-in Offered Price.

- Place the completed charts below the data table.

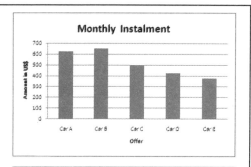

Improving the graphs

- The graphs presented above may not show clearly the right choice that meets Mrs Teo's need.

- You can further improve the graphs by drawing a line to indicate Mrs Teo's criterion.

- The notes below the graphs should help to indicate clearly the right choice.

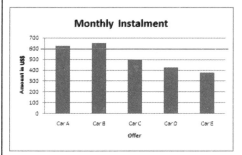

Only C, D & E meet the requirement of <$600

E is below the minimum trade-in offered price of $7000

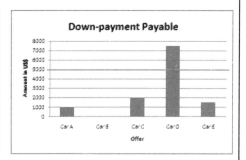

Down-payment payable for D is too high

Conditional formatting

- The spreadsheet can be further enhanced by using conditional formatting.

- For Column (d), the trade-in price offered ought to be above $7000. Set the format so that the figure will be in red once it is below 7000.

- Click on Home tab.

- Click **Conditional Formatting ▾**.

- In the second column, select **Less Than...**.

- In the third column, type 7000.

- Click **Format**.

- Select red for **Color:**.

  Select **Bold** for **Font style:**.

- Click **OK**.

- Click **OK** again.

- Cell D9 should now be displayed in red.

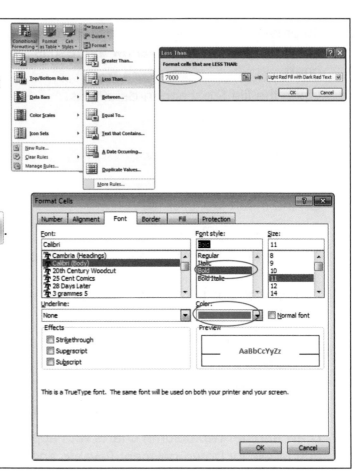

Columns (e) and (k)

- Repeat the conditional formatting for Column (e) where down-payment payable should not be more than $5000.

- Repeat the conditional formatting for Column (k) where the monthly instalment should not be more than $600.

- Once Mrs Teo's three criteria are indicated by conditional formatting, it is very obvious that Car C is the only offer that meets Mrs Teo's need.

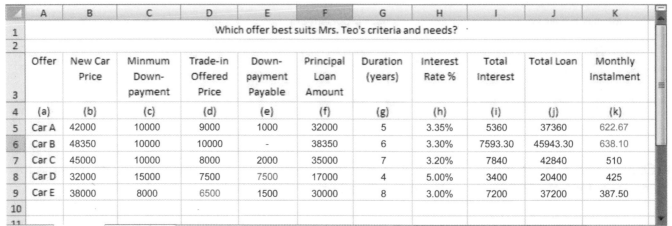

	A	B	C	D	E	F	G	H	I	J	K
1				Which offer best suits Mrs. Teo's criteria and needs?							
2											
3	Offer	New Car Price	Minmum Down-payment	Trade-in Offered Price	Down-payment Payable	Principal Loan Amount	Duration (years)	Interest Rate %	Total Interest	Total Loan	Monthly Instalment
4	(a)	(b)	(c)	(d)	(e)	(f)	(g)	(h)	(i)	(j)	(k)
5	Car A	42000	10000	9000	1000	32000	5	3.35%	5360	37360	622.67
6	Car B	48350	10000	10000	-	38350	6	3.30%	7593.30	45943.30	638.10
7	Car C	45000	10000	8000	2000	35000	7	3.20%	7840	42840	510
8	Car D	32000	15000	7500	7500	17000	4	5.00%	3400	20400	425
9	Car E	38000	8000	6500	1500	30000	8	3.00%	7200	37200	387.50
10											

More challenge

- Mrs Teo prefers Car A if only the monthly instalment can be reduced to less than $600!
- Mrs Teo is willing to pay more down-payment for Car A as long as the down-payment payable is less than $5000!
- Based on Mrs Teo's request, what is the down-payment payable, to the nearest $100, that Mrs Teo has to pay?
- Can you use the same spreadsheet to help Mrs Teo?
- Yes! For Column (c), the minimum down-payment in cell C5, change the value from 10 000 to 11 000.

- Check the value in Column (k), the monthly instalment.
- Does the value in cell K5 decrease to below 600?
- If not, increase the value for C5 to 11 100, 11 200, 11 300, ... until the value of K5 decreases to below 600.
- Write down the smallest value for C5 that helps to solve Mrs Teo's request:

_____

- Save the spreadsheet as Teo'scar-a.xlxs.

Evaluation

- Does the spreadsheet help to solve Mrs Teo's need?
  - Yes! The spreadsheet has shown Mrs Teo clearly that the offer that best suits her criteria is _____.
  - The spreadsheet can also be used to show Mrs Teo that by increasing the down-payment to $ _____, she can keep the instalment for Car A to below $600.

- What has been done to improve the spreadsheet so that the findings are clear?
  - The solution was presented using graphs.
  - The graphs were further improved by a red line that indicated the criteria.
  - The spreadsheet was also improved by the conditional formatting.

- Suggest other ways that may help to improve the spreadsheet so that it can meet its purpose.
  - Use colours to highlight the row that shows the solution.
  - Sort Column (k) – Monthly Instalment.
  - _____
  - _____
  - _____

Optional extension and challenge activities

Module 3 – Spreadsheets for a Purpose

Challenge 1

Who has the biggest handful?

- Create a spreadsheet to record the results of a science test, such as how many small plastic bricks different people can pick up with one hand.
- Make a bar chart of your results.
- What do you learn about the sizes of people's hands?

Challenge 2

Holiday spreadsheet

- Use the data to create a spreadsheet about the cost of different types of hotels and transport.

Hotel type	Cost per night US$	Cost hotel per week	Transport type	Cost per day US$	Cost transport per week	TOTAL cost per week
budget	30		bus	12		
mid range	40		train	25		
luxury	70		car	55		

- Insert 2 columns with formulas to find the cost of using each option for a week.
- Insert another column with a formula to find the total cost of using each option for a week.
- You have $500 to spend on your holiday. Which combinations of hotel and transport will let you stay within budget and have some spending money left?

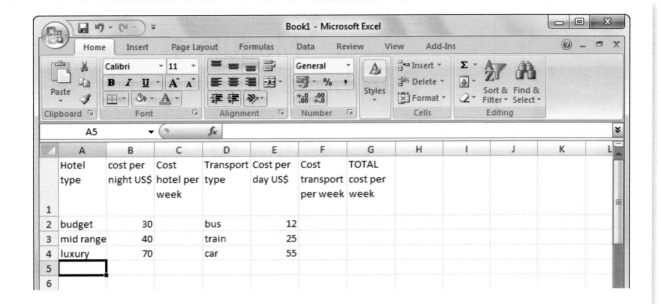

	A	B	C	D	E	F	G	H	I	J	K	L
1	Hotel type	cost per night US$	Cost hotel per week	Transport type	Cost per day US$	Cost transport per week	TOTAL cost per week					
2	budget	30		bus	12							
3	mid range	40		train	25							
4	luxury	70		car	55							
5												
6												

Challenge 3

- Use this data to find how many weeks each girl will have to save before she could buy each bike.

Type of bike	Cost in US$	Fatima saves $25 a week	Anna saves $40 a week	Lily saves $20 a week
Wheelie	500			
Atom	350			
Pedler	275			

Which bike could Lily buy before Fatima could buy an Atom?

What would Lily have to save each week to buy a Peddler in five weeks?

Module 4
Databases for a Purpose

Learning Objectives

	Student is able to:	Pass/Merit
1	Identify a purpose for a database	P
2	Design, create and develop a database for a specific purpose	P
3	Utilise different field types	P
4	Test database	M
5	Demonstrate an awareness of data security	M
6	Transfer data between applications	M

4.1 Databases

Designing databases

- A school computer club wants to collect data on the usage of the Internet among its members. You are asked to design a database to keep the data and to retrieve relevant information from time to time.
- The data collected will be kept confidential and only the main users, the Chairman, the Secretary and the Treasurer are allowed access.
- From the database collected, they would like to know:
  - the highest usage in hours per day
  - boys using dial-up connection
  - girls accessing the Internet for more than 3 hours.

- Discuss with your friends the key fields that are required and design a simple data entry form to be distributed to the members of the school computer club.
- The following are some examples of key fields:
  - Member ID
  - Name
  - Sex
  - Age
  - Type of connection to Internet (dial-up or broadband)
  - Average daily usage in hours
  - Date first subscribed to Internet Service Provider (ISP).

Data entry form

- Design a simple data entry form to be distributed to the members to collect data from them.

Computer Club
Sri Mawar Primary School
Survey on Internet Usage at Home

a. Member ID: _____

b. Name: _____   _____

c. Sex: _____   (Write M for Male and F for Female)

d. Age: _____

e. Type of connection to Internet: _____   (Write D for Dial-up, B for Broadband, and O for Other)

f. Average daily usage: _____ hours

g. Date first subscribed to ISP:____ / ____/ _____(DD/MM/YYYY)

_____   _____
   (Signature)   (Date)

Data structure

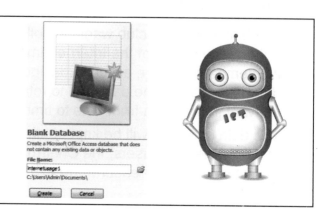

- Click 🌐 to open Start menu.
- Click ▶ **All Programs**.
- Click 🗗 **Microsoft Office Access 2007**.
- Click 🗐 **Blank Database**.
- Select your own directory or folder.
- Type internetusage1 as the filename.
- Click **Create** to create the database.

Creating a table

- Under the create tab, click 🗐 **Table**.

- Click on the arrow below 🗐 **View**, click 🖉 **Design View**
  and enter a name for the taste you are about to
  create. Click **OK**.

- Set up the table with the following details/options.

Field Name	Data Type	Field Properties
MemberID	Text	3
Name of member	Text	50
Sex	Text	1
Age	Number	Long Integer
Connection	Text	1
Usage	Number	Decimal
Date Subscribed	Date/Time	-

For the field Usage, set the decimal places to 1.

Data type

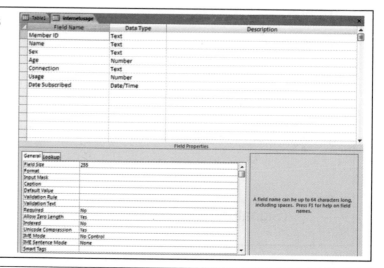

- The data type determines the kind of values
  that users can store in the field.
  - Text – Text or combination of text and
    numbers, including numbers that do not
    require calculation.
  - Memo – Lengthy text or combinations of
    text and numbers.
  - Number – Numeric data used in
    calculations.
  - Date/Time – Date and time values.
  - Currency – Currency values and
    numeric data used in calculations.

Primary key

- A good and effective database should include a field or set of fields that uniquely identifies each record stored in the table. This information is called the primary key of the table. Once you set a primary key for a table, Access will prevent any duplicate or null values from being entered in the primary key fields.

- Select the field MemberID and click 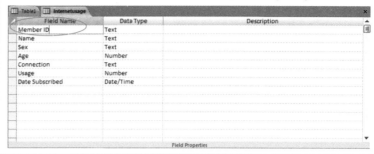 at the menu toolbar.

- A small key icon will appear in the Tools group on the Design tab, indicating that the field has been set as the primary key.

Saving the table

- Click to open Office menu.

- Click Save As and select Save Object As (Save the current database object as a new object).

- Save the table as internetusage.

- Click OK.

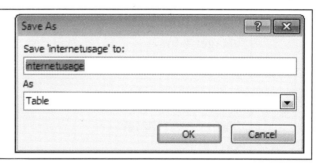

Entering data

- Click to select the table Internet Usage.

- Key-in the given data.

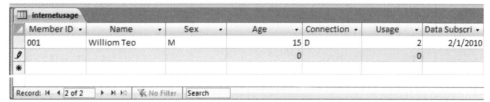

- To ensure data consistency, you will only enter Sex as M or F and enter connection as B for Broadband, D for Dial-up and O for Other.

- The format of data entered must be consistent. Dial-up is considered different from Dial up; Broad Band differs from Broadband.

MemberID: 001
Name: William Teo
Sex: M
Age: 15
Connection: D
Usage: 2.5 hrs
Date Subscribed: 02/01/2010

MemberID: 002
Name: Phua Chu Meng
Sex: M
Age: 16
Connection: B
Usage: 5 hrs
Date Subscribed: 01/07/2010

Record 3 to 12

MemberID: 003
Name: Elizabeth Goh
Sex: F
Age: 13
Connection: B
Usage: 8 hrs
Date Subscribed: 15/02/2012

MemberID: 004
Name: Mohad. Aziz
Sex: M
Age: 17
Connection: D
Usage: 1 hrs
Date Subscribed: 31/12/2011

MemberID: 005
Name: Mary Peter
Sex: F
Age: 16
Connection: D
Usage: 4 hrs
Date Subscribed: 07/05/2009

MemberID: 006
Name: Fatimah Ali
Sex: F
Age: 12
Connection: B
Usage: 5 hrs
Date Subscribed: 15/12/2012

MemberID: 007
Name: Siti Noraliza
Sex: F
Age: 15
Connection: D
Usage: 5 hrs
Date Subscribed: 01/02/2009

MemberID: 008
Name: Limalawati Hassan
Sex: F
Age: 16
Connection: D
Usage: 2 hrs
Date Subscribed: 03/08/2008

MemberID: 009
Name: Bruce Lee
Sex: M
Age: 17
Connection: B
Usage: 8 hrs
Date Subscribed: 01/03/2012

MemberID: 010
Name: Jong Ah Lai
Sex: M
Age: 14
Connection: B
Usage: 8 hrs
Date Subscribed: 15/06/2011

MemberID: 011
Name: Betty Victoria
Sex: F
Age: 15
Connection: B
Usage: 7 hrs
Date Subscribed: 18/11/2011

MemberID: 012
Name: Henry Joseph
Sex: M
Age: 16
Connection: B
Usage: 6.5 hrs
Date Subscribed: 19/10/2011

Records 13, 14 and 15

MemberID: 013
Name: Boniface David
Sex: M
Age: 16
Connection: D
Usage: 1 hrs
Date Subscribed: 15/09/2010

MemberID: 014
Name: Anthony Yap
Sex: M
Age: 12
Connection: B
Usage: 6 hrs
Date Subscribed: 08/08/2011

MemberID: 015
Name: Lai Fatt Cai
Sex: M
Age: 15
Connection: B
Usage: 6 hrs
Date Subscribed: 05/12/2011

Retrieve information

- Supply the information required when you were first asked to set up the database.
- The first information:
  The highest usage in hours per day.
- This information can be retrieved easily.
- Open the table.
- Click any cell in the column Usage.
- Click $\begin{smallmatrix} Z \\ A \end{smallmatrix}\downarrow$ to sort the data in descending order.
- After sorting, the number that appears at the top indicates the highest usage in hours, that is, 8 hours.

Member ID	Name	Sex	Age	Connection	Usage	Date Subscri
010	Jong Ah Lai	M	14	B	8	6/15/2011
009	Bruce Lee	M	17	B	8	1/3/2012
003	Elizabeth Goh	F	13	B	8	2/15/2012
011	Betty Victoria	F	15	B	7	11/18/2011
012	Henry Joseph	M	16	B	6	10/19/2011
015	Lai Fat Cai	M	15	B	6	5/12/2011
014	Anthony Yap	M	12	B	6	4/8/2011
007	Siti Noraliza	F	15	D	5	1/2/2009
006	Fatimah Ali	F	12	B	5	12/15/2012
002	Phua Chu Meng	M	16	B	5	1/7/2010
005	Mary Peter	F	16	D	4	7/5/2009
001	William Teo	M	15	D	2	2/1/2010
008	Liamalawati Hassan	F	16	D	2	3/8/2008
013	Boniface David	M	16	D	1	9/15/2010
004	Mohd. Aziz	M	17	D	1	12/31/2011

Record: ◄ ◄ 1 of 15 ► ►I ►☆ No Filter Search

Num Lock

Using a filter

- You can create a filter to find the information on:
  Boys that use dial-up connection.
- On the Home tab, in the Sort & Filter group, click
  Advanced ▾.
- Click Filter By Form.
- Select M in the column Sex.
- Select D in the column Connection.

Member ID	Name	Sex	Age	Connection	Usage	Data Subscri
001	William Teo	M	15	D	2.5	2/1/2010
004	Boniface David	M	16	B	5	9/15/2010
013	Mohd. Aziz	M	17	D	1	12/31/2011

Record: ◄ ◄ 4 of 4 ► ►I ►☆ Filtered Search

- Click Toggle Filter to apply the filter and then
  click Toggle Filter again to see all the records.

Query

- Create a query for the third information required: Girls that access the Internet for more than 3 hours.
- Close the table by clicking on the ☒ on the right hand side of the table.

- On the Create tab, in the Other group, click
- Choose `Simple Query Wizard` and click `OK`.
- Click `>>` to select all the fields.
- Click `Next >`.

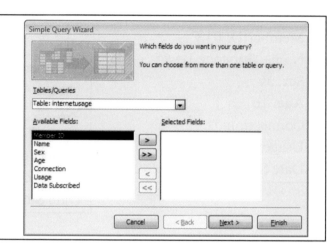

Simple Query Wizard

- Click `⦿ Detail (shows every field of every record)`.
- Click `Next >`.

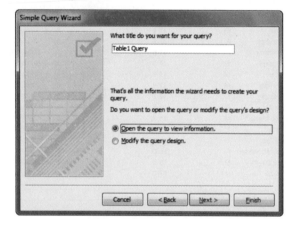

- Type internetusagequery-girlsuse>3h as the name of the query.
- Click `⦿ Modify the query design.`.
- Click `Finish`.

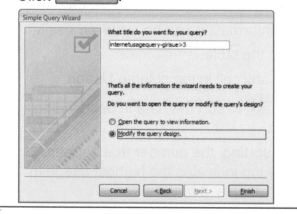

Change the query

- In the column Sex, type "F".
- In the column Usage, type >3.
- Click ▮ to run the query.

  Run

I also spend more than 3 hours surfing the net every day!

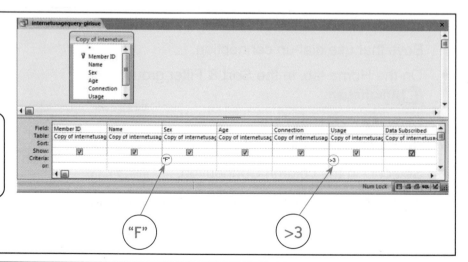

"F"   >3

Result of query

- The result of the query shows that there are 5 girls who use the Internet for more than 3 hours every day!

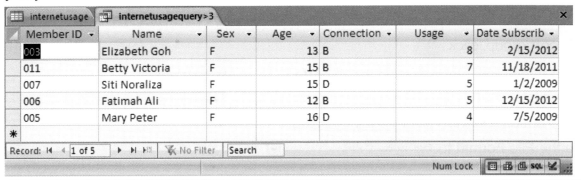

Other queries

- You can always change the query for other information.

- Find out:

  Who are still using dial-up connection?

- Select internetusage Query – girls use>3h and click 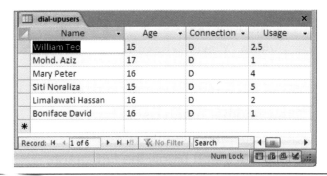 Design View .

- Delete the criteria in the columns Sex and Usage.

- Type D in the column Connection in the row for Criteria.

- Uncheck the check-box for the fields MemberID, Sex and Date Subscribed so

that we have information on Name, Age, Connection and Usage only.

- Save the query as dial-upusers.

- Click to run the query.

  Run

Queries exercises

- Create a new query using the Query Wizard to search for information on:
  - The Broadband users; save the query as broadbandusers.
  - Boys who are more than 15 years old and used the Internet for more than 5 hours; save your query as boys>15yrs>5h.
  - Users who are less than 14 years old; save your query as youngusers.

- Change the broadbandusers query to find out who used Broadband before the year 2005; save the query with a suitable name.

  (Hint: type <#01/01/2012# in the column Date Subscribed for Criteria)

- Modify the boys>15yrs>5h query to find out girls who are more than 16 years old and use the Internet or more than 4 hours; save the query with a suitable name.

- Modify the youngusers query to find out who use the Internet for more than 7 hours per day; save the query as heavyusers.

Export to MS Excel

- Open the query dial-upusers from the previous exercise.
- Click on External Data tab.
- In the Export group, click Excel.
- Select the folder you intend to save the exported information in.
- Check the option Export data with formatting and layout.
- Change the File Format to Excel Workbook (*.xlsx).
- Click OK.

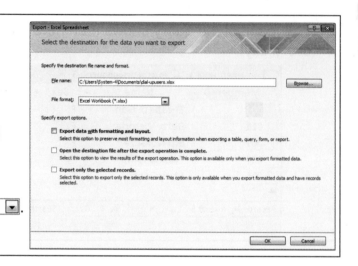

Graph in MS Excel

- Load Microsoft Office Excel 2007.
- Open the file dial-upusers.xlxs.
- Plot a column chart on Dial-up Users by Usage with:
  - Chart title: Dial-up Users
  - Category (X-axis): Names
  - Value (Y-axis): Usage Per Day in Hours.
- Remove the legend.
- Place the graph under the data table.
- Draw another graph Users by Age.
- Use a suitable title and labels.
- Place the graph below the first graph.

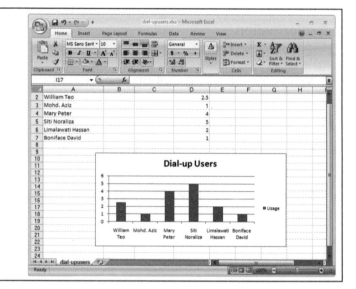

Export to MS Word

- Change the broadbandusers query so that it shows only Broadband users who are less than 15 years old.
- Save the query as bb_below15yrs.
- Click on External Data tab.
- In the Export group, click Word.
- Select the folder you intend to save the exported information in.
- Click OK.

- The file is saved as as type
  C:\Users\System-4\Desktop\Rich Text Format.rtf
- You can save it again in the docx format.

Name	Sex	Age
Phua Chu Meng	M	16
Elizabeth	F	13
Fatimah Ali	F	12
Bruce Lee	M	17
Jong Ah Lai	M	14
Betty Victoria	F	15
Henry Joseph	M	16
Anthony Yap	M	12
Lai Fatt Cai	M	15

Data back-up

- To prevent loss of data, you must always save back-up copies of the database.
- You can use the same filename or a new filename.
- Save the file in other storage devices like USB thumb or pen drive, CD or any other suitable devices.
- The back-up files must not be stored in the same room as the original data files.

For very important database, like in banks, the back-up files are even kept in a separate building to prevent data loss in case of fire!

Database password

- Passwords can be used to prevent unauthorised persons from reading the data.
- Before you can apply a database password, the database must be opened in the Exclusive mode.
- Select internetusage.accdb from the folder.
- Click on Database Tools tab.
- Click **Encrypt with Password**.
- Type a password of your own choice.
- Retype the exact password to verify.
- Click **OK**.

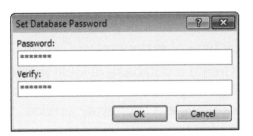

User and group Permissions

- Select internetusage.mdb file from the folder.
- In the Administrator group, click **Users and Permissions**.
- You can then set permissions for different users to access or perform different tasks to the table or queries.

You can apply user and group permissions to your database only when it has been saved as a .mdb file.

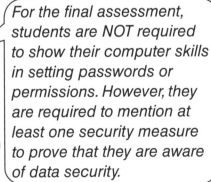

For the final assessment, students are NOT required to show their computer skills in setting passwords or permissions. However, they are required to mention at least one security measure to prove that they are aware of data security.

Optional extension and challenge activities

Module 4 – Databases for a Purpose

Challenge 1

Make a birthday database so you can see when and what to give your friends for special celebrations!

Create a database with fields for:

- Name
- Date of birth
- Girl / boy
- special interests
- What other fields might be useful?

Remember to be consistent when you input the data.

Challenge 2

What type of restaurant would you like to visit?

- Create a database of local restaurants which serve meals from different cultures. You might want to record how far they are from your home and if they deliver food or provide a take-away service.

Challenge 3

What local entertainments are there in your area? Are there cinemas, museums, sports facilities or clubs you can join?

- Make a database that supplies useful information and contact details for each one.
- Sort the records to see which facilities are closest to your home or which are the most expensive to use.